AF481337
LJ'S
INFLUENCE
A Young Man's Quest to Conquer Diabetes II in His Family
By Shawn Jenkins
MS, ATC, CSCS
Illustrator
Katie African

LJ's INFLUENCE

A Young Man's Quest to Conquer Diabetes II in His Family

Copyright © 2024 Stockton Sports Performance | Shawn Jenkins

Paperback ISBN 13: 979-8-8692-6655-2

Hardcover ISBN 13: 979-8-8692-5791-8

This book is dedicated to the memory of my mother, Mrs. Dee, whose unconditional love provided for and guided me in the right direction. I am forever grateful.

I am also grateful to my family who encourages me to be the best version of myself.

Thank you for your support.

LJ'S INFLUENCE

A Young Man's Quest to
Conquer Diabetes II in His Family

By Shawn Jenkins
MS, ATC, CSCS

Introduction

The family is preparing for their annual summer trip from Louisiana to the grandparent's home in East Oakland, California. One week into the vacation, Pop Pop is not feeling well, passes out and is rushed to the hospital where it is determined that he suffered from hyperglycemia (high blood sugar), a complication from having diabetes. LJ has many questions as he is introduced to diabetes and its impact on his family. After learning more about it and what is needed and how to avoid it, LJ is determined to help his Pop Pop. This new health awareness helps the rest of the family as well. They begin to implement practices which focus on healthier eating, exercise, and getting adequate amounts of sleep.

The day has FINALLY arrived! Joshua, affectionately called LJ by his family, hops out of bed and hurries to his little sister Dee's room to wake her. This is unusual because LJ normally has to be awakened by his mom, Cynthia. Once he enters Dee's room, LJ excitedly yells, "Get up and get ready! It's time to go visit Pop Pop and Ma Ma!" He heads to the kitchen where his mom is preparing a breakfast of pork sausage links, cheese eggs, white bread toast with grape jelly, and orange juice. LJ greets his mom, "Good morning!" and walks over to give her a hug.

"Hey LJ! Did you sleep well?"

"Yes, ma'am, I did. Where is dad?" asks LJ. "As a matter of fact, why don't you go wake him. Tell him breakfast will be ready soon."

LJ hurries toward his parent's room.

"Dad!" he yells, before getting to the door.
He knocks a few times before he hears
come in. LJ enters the room, and his dad,
Big Josh, is lying in bed, still groggy from
being awakened by his son.

"Wake up, dad!

Today is the day we are going to visit Pop Pop and Ma Ma, and mom says breakfast will be ready soon." Shortly thereafter, the family is enjoying a nice breakfast and discussing the plans for the day. After breakfast, LJ scampers to his room to finish packing his bag for the flight. An hour later, everyone is packed and ready to head off to the airport. Buckled in the back of the SUV, LJ and Dee are so excited that they find it difficult to sit still.

"How much longer?" LJ asks.

"We will arrive in 15 minutes," his mother responds.

Finally, they arrive at the parking lot and unload the car. There is no reason to rush because they have arrived with plenty of time to spare, but that doesn't mean much to LJ. "C'mon, ya'll; let's go!" he exclaims.

"Calm down, young man. We have plenty of time," his dad responds.

Big Josh and Cynthia hand their identification and boarding passes to the TSA agent who looks at LJ and asks, "Where are you headed, young man?" LJ excitedly replies, "We are going to visit my grandparents in Oakland, California!"

"That's awesome," the TSA agent replies.

"Have a good time!"

"Thank you, sir," says LJ as he proceeds to place his backpack on the belt to be examined. Now that they have made it through the security gates, Cynthia detours to the shop to grab a few snacks for the plane ride. "What would you like?" she asks LJ and Dee. "You each can choose one candy and a soda." LJ picks up a Snickers bar, Dee chooses Skittles, and Cynthia grabs Peanut M&Ms. They all head to the boarding gate where Big Josh is seated. After about an hour, which seems like forever to LJ, the family boards the plane and off

they go to Oakland. After a long flight, LJ is impatiently waiting for the other passengers to grab their bags. He can't wait to see Pop Pop, whom he loves dearly. Finally, the aisle is clear to disembark. Half walking, half jogging, LJ is ahead of the rest of his family. "Slow down!" his dad says loudly. LJ slows his steps but is still hurried. He reaches the escalator and waits for the rest of his family to arrive. Once the family reaches the bottom of the escalator, LJ sees Pop Pop entering the airport. LJ has a big smile on his face and asks his parents if he can go and greet Pop Pop. Dee follows after him.

Both run into the arms of their grandfather and they give each other a big hug. Once the rest of the family joins them and give each other hugs and kisses, they grab their luggage and head to the car.
Airport

On the way home, Pop Pop says, "Ma Ma is so excited to see all of you." They arrive at the grandparent's house, and head up the driveway where Ma Ma is standing in front of the house waving. LJ and Dee hop out of the car and give Ma Ma a big hug. Josh & Pop Pop unload the luggage and they all head into the house. Ma Ma tells them to go wash up and to prepare for dinner. She makes a dinner consisting of chicken smothered in gravy, mashed potatoes, and sweet peas with Red Velvet cake and vanilla ice cream for dessert. Everyone is full after a delicious dinner and heads to the family room to chat and allow their meal to digest.

After spending time catching up and sharing old stories, everyone prepares for bed to get some much needed sleep after such an exciting day.

The following morning, Big Josh and LJ are at the sporting goods store to purchase golf balls for tomorrow's golf outing. Big Josh's phone rings and it's his wife, Cynthia, telling him to get to the local hospital. Pop Pop passed out and has been transported there. Big Josh tells LJ they must leave and check on Pop Pop, who has become ill. They arrive and see Ma Ma, Cynthia, and Dee in the waiting room. "What happened to Pop?" Big Josh asked.

"We don't know yet," Cynthia replies. A few minutes later, the doctor arrives to update the family on Pop Pop's condition.

The doctor says Pop Pop has not been consistently taking his diabetes medication and suffered from his blood sugar level being too high.

LJ listens and at the same time looks puzzled about what he hears. He leans toward his mom and asks, "What is diabetes?"

"I'll explain later, dear," she responds. The doctor continues to explain to the family how important it is that Pop Pop takes his medication as directed and says that they will keep him in the hospital for a couple of days for observation and to be certain he is well enough to go home. "Can we go see him?" LJ eagerly asks. "You can," says the physician, "but don't stay too long. He needs to get some rest. It's part of the recovery process."

The family makes their way back to see Pop Pop. LJ nervously approaches the door where he

sees his Pop Pop lying in the hospital bed. LJ's little brown eyes begin to fill with tears. He is sad to see his grandfather in this condition.

Pop Pop says to LJ in a reassuring voice, "Hey, lil man. Don't worry, I will be fine. Come give me a hug."

LJ walks over and gives him a hug. It seems to make everything better. "Hey, old man," Big Josh says to his dad. "You know what this means when you're released? You must take this seriously and get on track. We don't want this scare again. We need to make some changes." "I know," says Pop Pop. After visiting for about thirty minutes, it is time to leave and allow Pop Pop to rest. LJ gives him a big hug once more before departing and says, "I love you, Pop Pop."

"I love you too, lil' man", he responds. The ride back to the house is quiet. Cynthia looks at LJ through the rearview mirror and can tell that he is worried and deep in thought.

Having finally arrived home, Ma Ma says she's going to prepare dinner and summons Cynthia and Dee to assist her. "Hey LJ," his dad calls out. "Let's chat. What's on your mind, son?"

"I'm worried about Pop Pop," LJ says.

"Will he be okay? What is diabetes? Will he die from it? Can he be cured?" Josh strokes the sides of his goatee as he ponders the best way to answer these questions from his young son. Big Josh begins to explain, "Diabetes is a condition where the body does not properly use food for energy. An organ called the pancreas makes a hormone called insulin which helps glucose, a substance in food, get into the cells for our body to use for activity."

"What is the pancreas?" LJ asks. "The pancreas is an organ that sends the hormone insulin to regulate the blood sugar," explains his dad. LJ then asks, "What is insulin?" Big Josh explains, "Insulin

is a hormone that regulates the amount of sugar in the blood. When insulin does not work properly, glucose remains in the bloodstream causing high blood sugar, which is known as hyperglycemia. This damages the body, causes symptoms, and complicates the diabetes. Pop Pop has had diabetes for several years and manages it with medication given by his physician. Apparently, your grandfather has not been taking his medication or following other preventative measures to control his diabetes."

Big Josh continued, "Pop Pop has Type 2 diabetes, the most common kind. There are actions he can take to significantly minimize it, even rid himself of the disease altogether, but he isn't doing what is necessary. Many people are diagnosed with Type 2 diabetes

due to poor eating habits, lack of exercise, and weight gain. If Pop Pop eats healthier, exercises regularly, and loses weight he can cure it."

LJ sits, absorbing the information his dad has provided, but still has more questions. He lifts his head from looking down at the porch and asks, "Will I have diabetes?" Big Josh tells him that it is not certain that he will. Big Josh tells LJ, "I have been diagnosed with pre-diabetes, and must take steps to make sure it doesn't become full diabetes." Cynthia arrives on the porch and joins the conversation.

"Son, there are certain risk factors that lead to Type 2 diabetes."

- Poor eating habits that lead to becoming overweight or being obese. When you have too much body fat your cells may become resistant to insulin.

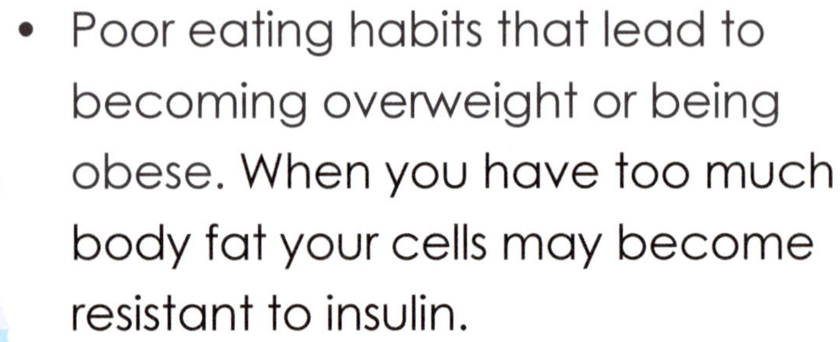

- Inactivity or the lack of regular exercise. The less active you are, the greater the risk.

- Family history/genetics.

"It's not necessarily certain that you will become diabetic, but there are some actions that you can take to decrease your chances of getting it. Son, I must make a better effort to take this more seriously to lessen the chance of getting diabetes by eating healthier, consistently exercising, and losing body fat. I don't want to be prescribed diabetes medication. Many individuals have demonstrated diabetes is curable by following a proper diet and frequent exercise routine. Ma Ma also has pre-diabetes but has avoided diabetes by consistently following her physician's orders of eating healthy foods and exercising. I must do better regarding my own health. This certainly has been a wake-up call."

LJ looks up at his father and mother and says with hope, "Sooo, there is something we can do to make Pop Pop better?"

His dad replies, "Absolutely, son!"

"Pop Pop comes home tomorrow?" asks LJ.

"If his diabetes numbers are under control and the doctor is satisfied with his progress, yes." his dad replies.

LJ asks his dad if he can use the laptop to learn more about diabetes. LJ is a very smart young man. He is the top student in his class.

His dad helps him with the research, reading articles and watching videos about how to avoid diabetes. Dee also joins them on the porch.

The day has arrived! Pop Pop has done well enough to be released from the hospital. Big Josh and Ma Ma leave to pick him up.

LJ, Dee, and their mom eagerly await his arrival. After some time, they see the car coming up the long driveway. Everyone runs to greet Pop Pop. "I'm soooo glad you're feeling better," LJ says as he gives his grandfather a big hug.

"Awww, thank you, grandson." "Son, your grandpa needs to get his rest," says Big Josh. "While he's resting, you and I can watch the ball game."

The game has reached half time and LJ tells his dad, "I have a plan to help Pop Pop."

"You do? What do you have in mind, son?" Josh asked. "The information on diabetes mentioned that a healthy diet and exercise can reverse the disease," LJ points out. "I want to make sure Pop Pop is doing the right things to get rid of this disease. We can make sure he is eating the proper foods and getting his daily exercises. We need to have a family meeting."

Big Josh summons the family to meet.

"Pop, we love you. The incident regarding your diabetes has really had an impact on LJ. A few of our family members are impacted by this disease as well. He has researched diabetes, learned what it is and how we can help you defeat it".

Pop Pop responds, "Wow, grandson! You did that for me? I know you're a smart kid. This is amazing!"

Big Josh continues. "We need to address it individually and for the family's well-being."

"Based on his research on diabetes, LJ has developed a plan that focuses on improvement in the areas of exercise, healthy eating, and also an adequate amount of sleep.

We start by daily walking, minimizing processed fast foods, and eating healthier whole foods."

Big Josh continues to speak and looks in Pop Pop's direction.

"Ma Ma told me that your eating habits are not the healthiest. You don't exercise regularly, spend too many hours sitting and watching TV."

Big Josh goes on to say, "We will start tomorrow morning by going for a walk. Afterwards, clean out the pantry to eliminate foods that are not beneficial to your health. This is your new lifestyle.

There are foods you will need to minimize or eliminate if you want to avoid another trip to the hospital. Food and beverages containing excess sugar must be minimized or avoided. Minimize your intake of high fat meats, especially processed meats such as bacon,

hot dogs, deli lunch meat. Don't overeat." After listening to the recommendations, Pop Pop agrees to follow the plan.

Ma Ma prepares a nutritious breakfast consisting of oatmeal with blueberries, turkey patties, eggs with spinach, almond milk, and orange juice. Every morning after breakfast, the entire family goes for a walk for at least thirty minutes.

They gradually add resistance training to strengthen the muscles which has proven to also improve balance and brain activity.

After walking, Pop Pop, Big Josh, and LJ retreat to the family room to relax. Big Josh says to his dad,

"Your hyperglycemic (high blood sugar) incident has resulted in something positive."

Josh explained further, "Because he loves his Pop Pop, your smart grandson researched what diabetes is and what steps can be taken to control and eventually get rid of it. LJ's influence also helped other pre-diabetic family members, who must make the necessary changes to avoid a full-blown diabetes diagnosis." Big Josh pulled LJ aside. "Son, I want you to know how proud I am that you took the initiative to learn about diabetes and how to help Pop Pop and the rest of the family. You have made a big difference and have positively influenced this family's health.

I love you, son!" That evening, the family dinner was much healthier. More vegetables, baked lean meats, and no sodas or other high sugar beverages.

After eight weeks of healthier eating, exercising, and getting adequate sleep, it was time for a follow-up appointment with the doctor. The following week, Big Josh and Ma Ma accompany Pop Pop to his appointment.

After several tests, the results were in. The doctor enters the room with a slight grin. "Well, Mr. Griffin, based on your results, you've been doing an outstanding job! Your glucose (blood sugar) and cholesterol levels have not looked this good in five years. You have lost 20 pounds and your blood pressure is within the normal range. Congratulations! What is your secret?" asked the doctor. Pop Pop responded, "There is no secret. Doc, it's about love. After that medical scare with my diabetes, my grandson, LJ, wanted to do something to help me. He developed a plan of eating healthier, exercising frequently, and getting an adequate amount of sleep. He made sure I stayed on task. It is a challenge in the beginning. Because I know he loves me and I love him, I wanted to do the right thing. I am glad I did, and I feel much better since following the program."

"Excellent," said the doctor. "Keep following the program and make an appointment to see me in three months."

The car ride back to the house was joyous. Pop Pop received good news from the doctor and is further encouraged to continue with his new lifestyle.

After arriving home, Pop Pop summoned LJ's attention. "Grandson, I thank you for taking the lead on getting all of us on track with our health. I took it for granted and paid the price. I appreciate your intelligence, determination, and most of all, the love you demonstrated toward your family. I love you."

As you have just read, LJ made a huge impact on the lives of his family. He recognized the issue, researched how to improve the situation, developed a plan, and put that plan into action. You can do the same. If you have family members or friends who have pre-diabetes, diabetes, or other health issues and are not focused on improving them, ask them why not? Just like LJ, you can have influence as well.

Do like LJ. In the end, it's all about love. Just like the love LJ has for his Pop Pop and the rest of the family.

Best Practices for Combating Diabetes

The following items must be put into action when adopting in a healthy lifestyle aimed to avoiding diabetes.

Nutrition

To function effectively, and efficiently, you must properly fuel your body for activity. Overeating and fueling up on processed foods, high in salt, sugar and bad fats is the incorrect approach.

You must eat healthier to address your diabetic condition or avoid it. This will include:

- Fruits

- Vegetables

- Whole grains (complex carbohydrates)

    ◊ Barley, brown rice, buckwheat, bulgur, millet, oatmeal, popcorn, whole wheat bread, pasta, or crackers.

- Legumes, such as beans and peas.

- Low-fat dairy products, such as milk, yogurt, and cheese.

Fiber

Eat food with more fiber. Fiber helps control blood sugar levels. Foods high in fiber are:

- Vegetables

- Fruits

- Nuts

- Legumes, such as beans and peas

- Whole grains

Protein

Eating fish such as salmon, mackerel, tuna, and sardines are rich in omega-3 fatty acids. These meats are good for the

heart. Other meats to consider are chicken, turkey, beef, veal, lamb, bison, goat, lean pork, beef liver, whole eggs, and beans or legumes.

Fats

- Oils: Avocado, Olive, Canola, Flaxseed, Walnut, Sesame, Grapeseed, and Sunflower

  AVOID: Coconut, partially hydrogenated, and palm oils

- Nuts

- Dark chocolate

Dairy

- Low fat sources of milk, yogurt, cheese

- Lactose intolerance options: soy, non-dairy sources (oat milk or almond milk), or take a lactose enzyme pill.

Avoid or Minimize

Less healthy carbohydrates, sodas, processed foods, foods or drinks with added fats, sugars, high sodium, high fructose corn syrup, saturated fats, and trans fats.

Diabetes increases your risk of heart disease and stroke by accelerating the development of clogged and hardened arteries. Frequently eating foods poor in nutrition and not exercising works against a heart-healthy diet.

The following foods are not helpful in maintaining a healthy heart and should be minimized.

- **Saturated fats.** Avoid or minimize high-fat dairy products and animal proteins such as hot dogs, sausage, and bacon. Also limit coconut and palm kernel oils.

- **Trans fats.** Avoid trans fats found in processed snacks, baked goods, shortening, and stick margarines.

- **Cholesterol.** Cholesterol sources include high-fat dairy products and high-fat animal proteins. Aim for no more than 200 milligrams (mg) of cholesterol a day.

- **Sodium.** Aim for less than 2,300 mg of sodium a day. Your doctor may suggest you aim for even less if you have high blood pressure.

https://www.mayoclinic.org/diseases-conditions/diabetes/in-depth/diabetes-diet/art-20044295

Exercise

The Center for Disease Control (CDC) recommends 150 minutes per week of moderate exercise, such as brisk walking, and 30 minutes a day or 75 minutes per week of rigorous activity, such as running. It is also advised to take part in muscle building activities, such as lifting weights/resistance training, at least 2 days a week.

Preparing for Bedtime

Sleep is also very important in the battle against diabetes. Poor sleeping habits lead to higher levels of stress hormones which can cause blood sugars to run high. Abnormal sleep results in higher levels of resting stress hormones like epinephrine, norepinephrine, as well as cortisol, and then those stress hormones can influence blood sugar control. Get an adequate amount of sleep. Shut down your cell phone and video games early and get at least 8 hours of sleep.

As you can see, sleep is especially important to those with diabetes. A couple of suggestions before going to bed:

- Don't overeat or drink high sugar beverages prior to bedtime.

- Limiting screen time at night and artificial light is also important. If you're using your iPad or your computer or e-reader, that artificial light can disturb the way the body produces melatonin, a sleep hormone that's important for regulating sleep-wake cycles.

The End

About the Author

Shawn Jenkins, born and raised in East Oakland, California, is a Certified Strength and Conditioning Specialist and Certified Athletic Trainer with a Master's degree in Kinesiology and an American Council on Exercise (ACE) certification as a Fitness Nutrition Specialist.

He has a strong passion for empowering people to live productively through incorporating exercise and nutrition. Quick fixes or gimmick diets are not productive long-term. Shawn believes in equipping yourself with verified scientific information from credible sources, staying on course with this lifestyle to live as healthy as possible.